W9-DFS-153

"Fairest Star of All"

"FAIREST STAR OF ALL"

A LITTLE TREASURY

Compiled by

ST. ANTHONY GUILD PRESS

"FAIREST STAR OF ALL"

≠

OF MARIOLOGY

Francis Edward Nugent

PATERSON, NEW JERSEY 1956

Nihil obstat:

BEDE BABO, O. S. B.,

Censor librorum.

Imprimatur:

† JAMES A. MCNULTY,

Bishop of Paterson.

April 2, 1956

PRINTED IN THE UNITED STATES OF AMERICA

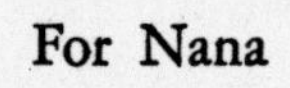
For Nana

A NOTE ON SOURCES

Excerpts in this anthology are taken from well-known works of early Christian, medieval and modern times including: St. Augustine, *Lib. de sancta Virginitate,* cap. xii (Nos. 77, 107, in this book), *De natura et gratia,* xxvi (No. 108), St. Augustine as cited in Newman's *Letter to Pusey* (No. 45); Hilaire Belloc, "Ballade to Our Lady of Czestochowa" (No. 94); Benedict XIV, *Gloriosae Dominae* (No. 95); Benedict XV, *Inter sodalicia* (No. 98); St. Bernard of Clairvaux, *On the Glories of the Virgin Mother* (Nos. 5, 60, 64, 82, 125, 127, 159, 160, 190, 199), *De Aquaeductu* (Nos. 100, 101); Monsignor Hugh F. Blunt, *Mary's Garden of Roses* (Nos. 29, 168, 212); Boccaccio, *Decameron* (No. 140); *Revelations* of St. Bridget of Sweden (Nos. 90, 91, 163); Chaucer, *Canterbury Tales* (Nos. 74, 145); Henry Constable, *Diana* (No. 73); Dante Alighieri, *Paradiso,* canto xxxiii (Nos. 72, 92), canto xxxii (No. 213); St. Ephrem, *Oratio ad Deiparam* (No. 157); Frederick William Faber, *Hymns* (No. 170), *Poems* (No. 193); St. Fulgentius, *De laudibus Mariae ex partu Salvatoris* (No. 124); Jean Guitton, *The Virgin Mary* (No. 220).

Right Reverend John C. Hedley, *The Christian Inheritance* (No. 24); Gerard Manley Hopkins, S. J., *Rosa Mystica* (No. 154); Caryll Houselander, *The Reed of God* (Nos. 156, 197, 198); Marigold Hunt, *Gospel Rhymes* (No. 184); St. Irenaeus, *Adversus Haereses* (No. 47); Mrs. Anna B. M. Jameson, *Legends of Monastic Orders* (No. 43); St. Jerome, as cited in Newman's *Letter to Pusey* (No. 45); St. John Damascene, *Homiliae duae de dormitione Virg. Mariae* (No. 56); Joyce Kilmer,*The Rosary* (No. 225); Rudyard Kipling, *Song before Action* (No. 155); Monsignor Ronald Knox, *Retreat for Priests* (Nos. 27, 68); William E. H. Lecky, *History of European Morals* (No. 41); *History of Rationalism,* Vol. I (No. 42); Edward Leen, C. S. Sp., *In the Likeness of Christ* (No. 180); Leo XIII, *Octobri Mense* (No. 96), *On the Rosary* (No. 222); Henry Wadsworth Longfellow, *The Golden Legend* (No. 34); Vincent McNabb, O. P., *Mary of Nazareth* (Nos. 12, 13, 14, 15, 28, 49, 117, 205); Joseph Manton, C. Ss. R., *The Stable and the Star,* an address on "The Catholic Hour" (No. 137); François Mauriac, *The Stumbling Block* (No. 33); Thomas Merton, *Thirty Poems* (No.

138), *Figures for an Apocalypse* (No. 169); John Henry Cardinal Newman, *On the Fitness of the Glories of Mary* (Nos. 16, 65, 135, 186, 203), *The Glories of Mary for the Sake of Her Son* (No. 136), *The New Eve* (Nos. 17, 18, 209), *Letter to Pusey* (No. 19), *Verses* (No. 66), *Sermon Notes* (No. 116), *The Second Spring* (No. 134), *Difficulties of Anglicans* (No. 166), *Parochial and Plain Sermons* (No. 218).

Coventry Patmore, *The Child's Purchase* (Nos. 25, 93); Petrarch, *Canzoniere* (No. 141); Pius IX, *Ineffabilis Deus* (Nos. 50, 208); Pius X, *Ad Diem Illum* (Nos. 1, 2, 97, 192, 216); Pius XII, *De S. Virginitate,* c. 6 (No. 76); Agnes Repplier, *Le Repos en Egypte* (No. 179); John Ruskin, *Sesame and Lilies* (Nos. 39, 40); St. Thomas Aquinas, *Summa theologica,* III, q. 27, a. 5 (No. 3), III, q. 25, a. 2 (Nos. 6, 61), III, q. 30, a. 2 (No. 11), III, q. 27, a. 4 (No. 109); III, q. 28, a. 2 (No. 113); Thomas a Kempis, reputed author of *The Imitation of Mary* (No. 133); Frank Sheed, *The Mary Book* (No. 167); Patrick Augustine Sheehan, *Under the Cedars and the Stars* (Nos. 70, 119, 183, 194, 204); Most Reverend Fulton Sheen, *The World's First Love* (Nos. 22, 23, 26, 30, 69, 120, 223); John Bannister Tabb, *Poetry of Father Tabb* (Nos. 174, 196); Tertullian, *De Carne Christi* (No. 48); Francis Thompson, *The After Woman* (No. 139), *To a Dead Astronomer* (No. 153); Gerald Vann, O. P., *The Seven Swords* (No. 118); Anscar Vonier, O. S. B., *The Divine Motherhood* (No. 195); William Wordsworth, *Sonnet to the Virgin* (No. 121).

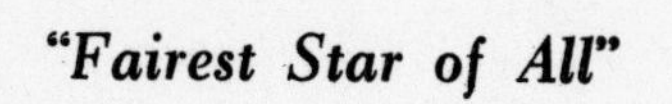
"Fairest Star of All"

What saidst thou, astronomer,
When thou didst discover her?
When thy hand its tube let fall
Thou found'st the fairest Star of all!

— FRANCIS THOMPSON, *To a Dead Astronomer*

Other Works by Francis Edward Nugent

ANTHOLOGIES:

A Spiritual Reader

The Priest in Our Day

A Father McNabb Reader

Saints Alive

First Epistles to Robert

1. *The Child is not found without Mary His Mother.*

ST. PIUS X

2. *True devotion to Christ demands true devotion to Mary.*

ST. PIUS X

3. *The nearer a thing approaches to its principle the more does it partake of the effect of that principle. But Christ is the principle of grace, and Mary is nearest to Him, since He received from her His human nature. Hence she ought to receive from Christ a greater fullness of grace than anyone else.*

ST. THOMAS AQUINAS

4. *As mariners are guided into port by the shining of a star, so Christians are guided to Heaven by Mary.*

ST. THOMAS AQUINAS

5. *The Word is coming, but Mary is the way whereby He comes.*

ST. BERNARD

6. *God's mother is our mother, too. The mother of Him in whom alone we hope, whom alone we fear, is our mother. We have for our mother the mother of Him who alone can save us, who alone will be our judge.*

ST. ANSELM

7. *If anyone does not profess that Emmanuel is truly God, and that consequently the Holy Virgin is the Mother of God—inasmuch as she gave birth in the flesh to the Word of God made flesh, according to what is written: "The Word was made flesh"—let him be anathema.*

DEFINITION OF THE COUNCIL OF EPHESUS (431)

8. *Mary is a sweet bait God has prepared to catch the hearts of men.*

ST. CATHERINE OF SIENA

9. *She was made the Mother of God more for sinners than for the just.*

ST. ANSELM

10. *I wish to go to Jerusalem, if you will permit me, to see the holy faithful who are there,*

especially Mary, the Mother of Jesus, who is said to be admired and loved by all. For what friend of our faith . . . would not be delighted to see and speak to her who brought forth the true God?

ST. IGNATIUS OF ANTIOCH
(writing to St. John the Evangelist)

11. *At the Annunciation the Virgin was asked to give her consent in the name of the whole human race.*

ST. THOMAS AQUINAS

12. *Our Lady is not a rival to her Son. The best background for gold is silver. The best background for silver is gold. A man may hold the moon to be a rival to the sun until he knows that the moon's light is but a loan from the sun.*

VINCENT McNABB, O. P.

13. *When a feast of Our Blessed Lady occurs, never be misled into thinking mainly of Our Blessed Lady. Keep the eye of your mind on her Divine Son. It is there she would have you look. It is there she herself is looking.*

VINCENT McNABB, O. P.

14. *Honoring Our Lady in no way takes away from the worship of God. The century that saw English ministers expanding their arms to receive fairy-like Lady-chapels, saw English hands flashing the sword or drawing the bow to win from the Saracen the home of Jesus Christ.*

VINCENT McNABB, O. P.

15. *Of people who see Our Lady mainly as a stumbling block:*

To me it is as if they said, "The chief stumbling block to my believing in the sun is the existence of the moon."

VINCENT McNABB, O. P.

16. *It is the boast of the Catholic religion that it has the gift of making the young heart chaste; and why is this but that it gives us Jesus Christ for our food, and Mary for our nursing Mother?*

JOHN HENRY CARDINAL NEWMAN

17. *He who charges us with making Mary a divinity is thereby denying the divinity of Jesus. Such a man does not know what divinity is.*

JOHN HENRY CARDINAL NEWMAN

18. *If it be idolatry in us to let our affections respond to our faith, He would not have made her what she is, or He would not have told us that He had so made her; but far from this, He has sent His Prophet to announce to us, "A Virgin shall conceive and bear a son, and they shall call His name Emmanuel," and we have the same warrant for hailing her as God's Mother as we have for adoring Him as God.*

JOHN HENRY CARDINAL NEWMAN

19. *If, as St. Irenaeus says, she acted the part of an Advocate, a friend in need, even in her mortal life; if, as St. Jerome and St. Ambrose say, she was on earth the great pattern of virgins; if she had a meritorius share in bringing about our redemption; if her maternity was gained by her faith and obedience; if her Divine Son was subject to her; and if she stood by the Cross with a mother's heart and drank in to the full those sufferings which it was her portion to gaze upon, it is impossible that we should not associate these characteristics of her life on earth with her present state of blessedness; and this surely she anticipated when she said in her hymn that all generations should call her blessed.*

JOHN HENRY CARDINAL NEWMAN

20. *Her sanctity comes not only of her being His Mother but also of His being her Son.*

JOHN HENRY CARDINAL NEWMAN

21. *By honoring Mary as Christ's Mother, Catholics can never forget that He is man; by constantly approaching Him through her mediation, they can never forget that He is God.*

WILLIAM GEORGE WARD

22. *The nature of her role is not to call her Son's attention to some need, in an emergency unnoticed by Him, nor is it to "win" a difficult consent. Rather, it is to unite herself to His compassionate mercy and give a human voice to His infinite love. The main ministry of Mary is to incline men's hearts to obedience to the will of her Divine Son.*

MOST REVEREND FULTON J. SHEEN

23. *As those who lose devotion to her lose belief in the divinity of Christ, so those who intensify devotion to her gradually acquire that belief.*

MOST REVEREND FULTON J. SHEEN

24. *To those who refuse to see His Mother, His own personality becomes dim and shadowy.*

RIGHT REVEREND
JOHN CUTHBERT HEDLEY, O. S. B.

25. [*Our Lady is*]

our only saviour from an abstract Christ.

COVENTRY PATMORE

26. *The one man who might be most inclined to doubt the historical fact of the virgin birth on natural grounds (because he was a physician) was the second Evangelist, St. Luke. And yet he tells us the most about it.*

MOST REVEREND FULTON J. SHEEN

27. *Protestants sometimes laugh at us because we address ourselves, now to Our Lady of Perpetual Succor, now to Our Lady of Good Counsel, now to Our Lady of Lourdes, and so on, as if they were so many different people. But the case is much worse than that, if they only knew; every individual Catholic has a separate "Our Lady" to pray to, his Mother, the one who seems to care for him individually, has won him so many*

favors, has stood by him in so many difficulties, as if she had no other thought or business in heaven but to watch over him.

MONSIGNOR RONALD KNOX

28. *I seem to see a reason why the Gospels do not mention any visit made by the risen Jesus to His Mother. There seems no doubt that the chief motive why Jesus stayed on earth forty days after His Resurrection was (a) to convince [His countrymen] that He had risen from the dead; and (b) to convince them that He forgave them even for putting Him to death. But Our Blessed Lady needed no reassurance on either of these two points.*

VINCENT McNABB, O. P.

29. *My own Mother always prayed for me when she was alive, and I know she is still praying for me in her corner of Heaven. So you do not need to tell me that my Heavenly Mother is not forgetting the obligation she assumed on Calvary of taking care of me forever.*

MONSIGNOR HUGH F. BLUNT

30. *If woman wants to be a revolutionist, then* THE WOMAN *is her guide, for she sang the most*

revolutionary song ever written — the Magnificat *— the burden of which was the abolition of principalities and powers, and the exaltation of the humble.*

MOST REVEREND FULTON J. SHEEN

31. *To assure our salvation it does not suffice to call ourselves children of Mary; therefore let us always have the fear of God.*

ST. TERESA OF AVILA

32. *Let Mary be held in honor. Let the Father, Son, and Holy Ghost be adored; but let no one adore Mary.*

ST. EPIPHANIUS

33. *It is absurd to imagine that what is not true can honor our Mother and please her, can fail to horrify her, even.*

FRANÇOIS MAURIAC

34. *And if our faith had given us nothing more than this example of all Womanhood, so mild, so merciful, so strong, so good, so patient, peaceful, loyal, loving, pure — this were enough to prove*

it higher and truer than all the creeds the world had known before.

HENRY WADSWORTH LONGFELLOW

35. *But I think His Mother will see me through.*

GEORGE BERNARD SHAW
(on confessing he could not believe
in the divinity of Christ)

36. *I have always envied the Catholics their faith in that sweet, sacred Virgin Mother, who stands between them and the Deity, intercepting somewhat of His awful splendor, but permitting His love to stream upon the worshiper more intelligibly to human comprehension through the medium of a woman's tenderness.*

NATHANIEL HAWTHORNE

37. *Lady most perfect, when thy sinless face*
Men look upon, they wish to be
A Catholic, Madonna fair, to worship thee!*

MARY LAMB

---

* The word *worship* is to be interpreted here as signifying the veneration we pay to Our Lady as the most perfect of mere human beings; and not as signifying divine worship, or that honor we pay to God alone.

38. *The worship* of the Virgin is to my mind — the mind of an unbeliever — full of holiness and beauty. We owe to it a great deal that is ennobling in life, in art, in literature.*

ROBERT BUCHANAN

39. *I am persuaded that the worship* of the Madonna has been one of the noblest and most vital graces, and has never been otherwise than productive of true holiness of life and purity of character.*

JOHN RUSKIN

40. *There has probably not been an innocent cottage home throughout the length and breadth of Europe, during the whole period of vital Christianity, in which the imagined presence of the Madonna has not given sanctity to the humblest duties, and comfort to the sorest trials of the lives of women; and every brightest and loftiest achievement of the arts and strength of manhood has been the fulfillment of the prophecy of the Israelite maiden: "He that is mighty hath magnified me and holy is His name!"*

JOHN RUSKIN

---

* See footnote on page 10.

41. *There is, I think, little doubt that the Catholic reverence for the Virgin has done much to elevate and purify the ideal of woman, and to soften the manners of men.*

WILLIAM EDWARD HARTPOLE LECKY

42. *No longer the slave or toy of man, no longer associated only with ideas of degradation and of sensuality, woman arose in the person of the Virgin Mother into a new sphere, and became the object of a reverential homage of which antiquity had had no conception.*

WILLIAM EDWARD HARTPOLE LECKY

43. *Through all the most beautiful and precious productions of human genius and human skill which the Middle Ages and Renaissance have bequeathed to us, we trace, more or less developed, more or less apparent, present in shape before us or suggested through inevitable associations, one prevailing idea; it is that of an impersonation in the feminine character of beneficence, purity and power, standing between an offended Deity and poor, sinning, suffering humanity and clothed in the visible form of Mary, the Mother of our Lord.*

ANNA BROWNELL MURPHY JAMESON

44. *Thy calm heart no breath hath shaken*
Of earth's passions; yet to thee
Come all they who have partaken
Of earth's utter misery.

GOETHE

45. *Death by Eve, life by Mary.*

ST. JEROME, ST. AUGUSTINE

46. *Adam from the virgin earth,*
Christ from a virgin.

ST. AMBROSE

47. *The knot of Eve's disobedience was untied through Mary's obedience, for what the virgin Eve tied by incredulity, the Virgin Mary unloosed by faith.*

ST. IRENAEUS

48. *Eve had believed the serpent; Mary believed Gabriel; the fault which the one committed by believing, the other by believing has blotted out.*

TERTULLIAN

49. *Eve was drawn from the side of Adam.*
Jesus was drawn from the womb of Mary.

VINCENT McNABB, O. P.

50. [*Quoting the Fathers of the Church in substance:*] *She approaches as near to God as created nature can, and she is far beyond all the praises of men and of angels.*

PIUS IX

51. *Such is the greatness of Mary, such the favor she has with God, that he who when in need of help would not run to her, would wish to fly without the aid of wings.*

LEO XIII

52. *The eternal Son of God, having willed to assume man's nature for his redemption and glory, and thereby to contract a mystic marriage with the whole human race, would not bring these espousals about until Mary, acting on behalf of humanity, had given her most free and untrammelled consent.*

LEO XIII

53. *Who can speak the praises of which Mary is worthy?*

ST. CYRIL OF ALEXANDRIA

54. [*Of her "Fiat":*]
By what homage can human frailty ever sufficiently acknowledge that it owes Heaven to thee!

ST. AUGUSTINE

55. *Thou hast been made more glorious, more pure, more saintly than all the rest of humankind.*

ST. GREGORY THAUMATURGUS

56. *All the tongues of men together could never celebrate Mary's praises worthily.*

ST. JOHN DAMASCENE

57. *As the light of the sun so greatly surpasses that of the stars that in it they are no longer visible, so does the great Virgin Mother surpass in sanctity the whole court of Heaven.*

ST. PETER DAMIAN

58. *Immediately next to being God is being the Mother of God.*

ST. ALBERT THE GREAT

59. *The prayers of the saints are the prayers of servants; but the prayers of Mary are prayers of a mother, and therefore they are regarded in a certain manner as commands by her Son, who loves her so tenderly. It is impossible that the prayers of Mary should be rejected.*

ST. ALPHONSUS LIGUORI

60. *The state to which God exalted Mary in making her His mother was the highest state which could be conferred on a pure creature; so that He could not have exalted her more.*

ST. BERNARD

61. *The Most Holy Virgin possesses, inasmuch as she is Mother of God, a dignity in some sort infinite on account of the Infinite Good to whom she is united; and in this regard she cannot be more highly exalted.*

ST. THOMAS AQUINAS

62. *All that is remarkable in any saint you will find in Mary: the patience of Job, the meekness of Moses, the faith of Abraham, the humility of David, the wisdom of Solomon, and the zeal of Elias.*

ST. THOMAS OF VILLANOVA

63. *God alone is above her; all that is not God is beneath her.*

ST. ANSELM

64. *The greatest glory, after God, is to see you, O Mary, to be close to you, and to repose under the shadow of your protection.*

ST. BERNARD

65. *Nothing is too high for her to whom God owes His human life; no exuberance of grace, no excess of glory but is becoming, but is to be expected there, where God has lodged Himself, whence God has issued.*

JOHN HENRY CARDINAL NEWMAN

66. [*Of Our Lady:*]

. . . I know of one work of His Infinite Hand,
which special and singular ever must stand,

So perfect, so pure, and of gifts such a store,
That even Omnipotence ne'er shall do more.

JOHN HENRY CARDINAL NEWMAN

67. *No more intimate union is to be found than that between God and the soul of Mary, except only the union between the two natures in Christ, and the unity of the Three Divine Persons.*

HERBERT ALFRED CARDINAL VAUGHAN

68. *Our Lady is the culmination of that long process of selection, of choosing here and rejecting there a human instrument suited to His purpose, which is so characteristic of God's dealings with His ancient people.*

MONSIGNOR RONALD KNOX

69. *Four instincts deeply embedded in the human heart [are]: affection for the beautiful; admiration for purity; reverence for a Queen; and love of a Mother. All of these come to a focus in Mary.*

MOST REVEREND FULTON J. SHEEN

70. *The Incarnation of our Lord Jesus Christ conferred upon His Mother a dignity proportioned to His humiliation. He humbled Himself, and she was exalted in the humiliation. He became man, and she became the Mother of God. The deeper He descended, the higher she ascended. He emptied Himself of His glory, and clothed her with it.*

PATRICK AUGUSTINE, CANON SHEEHAN

71. *Oh, Mary, God has chosen you and purified you, and elected you above all the women of the earth.*

THE KORAN

72. *In thee is mercy, in thee is pity; in thee are mighty deeds; in thee is united all the goodness that may in creature be.*

DANTE ALIGHIERI

73. *If men such high respect unto you bear,*
Which daughters, wives, and mothers are of
Kings,
What honor should unto that Queen be done
Who had your God for Father, Spouse and Son!

HENRY CONSTABLE

74. *Within the cloister blissful of thy sides*
Took man's shape the Eternal Love and Peace.

CHAUCER

75. *Nor shall her singing pass away.*
"He hath filled the hungry with good things" —
Oh, listen lords and ladies gay! —
"And the rich He hath sent empty away."

MARY COLERIDGE

76. *But when the little maid of Nazareth uttered her fiat to the message of the angel . . . she became not only the Mother of God in the physical order of nature; but also in the supernatural order of grace she became the Mother of all, who . . . would be made one under the headship of her Divine Son. The Mother of the Head would be the Mother of the members, the Mother of the vine the Mother of the branches.*

PIUS XII

77. *The Church is comparable to Mary; the Church is also virgin and mother, a fruitful virginity bringing forth the faithful members of Christ's Mystical Body.*

ST. AUGUSTINE

78. *In order to praise Mary it is enough to say that it is of her that Jesus was born.*

ST. THOMAS OF VILLANOVA

79. *After God, our greatest happiness is from her.*

ST. BONAVENTURE

80. *If Mary be for us, who shall be against us?*

ST. ANTONINUS OF FLORENCE

81. *Having confidence in you, O Mother of God, I shall be saved; being under your protection, I shall fear nothing; with your help, I shall give battle to my enemies and put them to flight; for devotion to you is an arm of salvation.*

ST. PETER DAMIAN

82. *Let us seek then for grace and seek it through Mary, for what she seeks she finds.*

ST. BERNARD

83. *O thou who feelest thyself tossed by the tempests of the world, turn not away thine eyes from the*

Star of the Sea, if thou wouldst avoid shipwreck. If the winds of temptation blow, if sufferings rise up like rocks before thee, a look at the star, a sigh towards Mary! If the waves of pride, ambition, calumny, jealousy seek to swallow up thy soul, a look towards the star, a prayer to Mary! If anger, avarice, love of pleasure splinter thy frail bark, seek the eyes of Mary! If horror of thy sins, trouble of conscience, dread of the judgments of God, begin to plunge thee into the gulf of sadness, the abyss of despair, attach thy heart to Mary! In thy dangers, thy anguish, thy doubts, think of Mary, call on Mary!

ST. BERNARD

84. *Let Mary be on thy lips, in thy heart.... Following her, thou canst not wander; whilst thou prayest to her, thou canst not be without hope; as long as thou thinkest of her, thou wilt be in the path; thou canst not fall when she sustains thee; thou hast nothing to fear while she protects thee; if she favor the voyage thou wilt reach safety's harbor without weariness.*

ST. BERNARD

85. *Devils flee before Mary's face as wax melts before the fire.*

ST. BONAVENTURE

86. *Whosoever bears the stamp of a servant of Mary is already enrolled in the Book of Life.*

ST. BONAVENTURE

87. *He who perseveres in Mary's service shall not be lost.*

ST. BONAVENTURE

88. *Glorious and wonderful is your name, O Mary; those who invoke it shall not tremble at the hour of death; for the devils retreat from the soul when they hear the name of Mary.*

ST. BONAVENTURE

89. *If thou protectest me, what can I fear? No, I fear nothing: I do not fear my sins, for thou canst provide a remedy: I do not fear devils, for thou art more powerful than the whole of Hell. I only fear lest in my temptations and by my own fault I may cease to recommend myself to thee and thus be lost.*

ST. ALPHONSUS LIGUORI

90. *I am the Mother of all the souls in Purgatory.*

OUR LADY, according to St. Bridget of Sweden

91. [*Our Lord to Our Lady, according to a vision of St. Bridget:*]

Because you have never denied Me anything on earth, I will deny you nothing in Heaven.

ST. BRIDGET OF SWEDEN

92. *So mighty art thou, Lady, and so great,*
That he who grace desireth, and comes not
To thee for aidance, fain would have desire
Fly without wings. Not only him who asks
Thy bounty succors; but doth freely oft
Forerun the asking.

DANTE ALIGHIERI

93. *Sunshiny peak of human personality.*

COVENTRY PATMORE

94. *Lady and Queen and Mystery manifold*
And very Regent of the untroubled sky.

HILAIRE BELLOC

95. *She is like a heavenly river upon whose flood all graces and gifts are borne to us unhappy mortals.*

BENEDICT XIV

96. *Just as no one can come to the Supreme Father except through the Son, so almost no one can come to Christ except through Mary.*

LEO XIII

97. *She administers the treasures of [Jesus'] merits as by a mother's right.*

ST. PIUS X

98. *It has pleased God to grant us all graces through the intercession of Mary.*

BENEDICT XV

99. *The Mother of God is the Ladder of Heaven. God came down by this ladder that men might, by Mary, climb up to Him in Heaven.*

ST. FULGENTIUS

100. *As every mandate of grace that is sent by a king passes through the palace gates, so does every grace that comes from Heaven to the world pass through the hands of Mary.*

ST. BERNARD

101. *God has placed the fullness of all gifts in Mary, so that if we find any grace, salvation, or hope we may be sure that it has flowed through her.*

ST. BERNARD

102. *God wills that all graces that have been, that are and will be dispensed to men to the end of the world through the merits of Christ, should be dispensed by the hands and through the intercession of Mary.*

ST. ALPHONSUS LIGUORI

103. *Every grace which is communicated to this world has a threefold course. . . . It is dispensed from God to Christ, from Christ to the Virgin, from the Virgin to us.*

ST. BERNARDINE OF SIENA

104. *When we have handled something fragrant, our hands perfume whatever we touch; let but our prayers pass through the hands of the Blessed Virgin, and she will give them fragrance.*

ST JOHN BAPTIST VIANNEY
(Curé d'Ars)

105. *Those who love Christ will not brook the assertion that the Mother of Christ ever ceased to be a virgin.*

ST. BASIL

106. *What man of sense could believe that the Son of God chose and made for Himself a living temple, an animated throne, wherein He was to be received, and that He was obliged to yield up the right and first use of it to the demon?*

ST. CYRIL OF ALEXANDRIA

107. *She conceived as a virgin, she gave birth as a virgin, she remained a virgin after childbirth. But why marvel at this? For God had so to be born if He condescended to become man.*

ST. AUGUSTINE

108. *When treating of sin I desire that, for the honor of Jesus Christ, no mention be made of Mary.*

ST. AUGUSTINE

109. *Mary would never have been worthy to be Mother of God had she committed a single sin.*

ST. THOMAS AQUINAS

110. *Other saints give example of particular virtues, but the Blessed Virgin gives examples of all.*

ST. THOMAS AQUINAS

111. *The virtues of Mary are the flowers that perfume the Church.*

ST. CASIMIR OF POLAND

112. *The rose without thorns, the white stainless lily, the Virgin, holy and adorned with the flowers of every virtue.*

ST. GERTRUDE

113. *Her purity, under Christ, was supreme.*

ST. THOMAS AQUINAS

114. *Virginal Lily, nod*
Gently thy jeweled brow
In the soft breath of God.

PETER ABELARD

115. *A Paradise of great beauty and perfection had been created for the angels. A Paradise was created for our first parents, a garden of delights proportioned to their nature. A Paradise*

was also created for the Incarnate Son of God — Mary most holy.

HERBERT ALFRED CARDINAL VAUGHAN

116. *She is the beautiful gift of God which outshines the fascinations of a bad world, and which no one ever sought in sincerity and was disappointed.*

JOHN HENRY CARDINAL NEWMAN

117. *Our Lady's purity was not snow but fire. It was the kindling purity of white heat, and not the chilling purity of white cold.*

VINCENT McNABB, O. P.

118. *Mary's life is a song at once of innocence and of experience.*

GERALD VANN, O. P.

119. *There is one thing remarkable in the definition of the Immaculate Conception. It was not forced upon the Church by a heresy, but it arose from the free, spontaneous will of her pastors and children, who spoke and acted as if there were a common feeling through Christendom that the dogmatic pronouncement of her Immaculate*

Conception, of her immunity from the great curse upon our race, was an honor to our Mother that had been too long delayed.

PATRICK AUGUSTINE, CANON SHEEHAN

120. *I never could see why anyone in this day and age should object to the Immaculate Conception; all modern pagans believe that they are immaculately conceived. If there is no original sin, then* everyone *is immaculately conceived. Why do they shrink from allowing to Mary what they attribute to themselves?*

MOST REVEREND FULTON J. SHEEN

121. *Mother! whose virgin bosom was uncrossed*
With the least shade of thought to sin allied;
Woman! above all women glorified —
Our tainted nature's solitary boast.

WILLIAM WORDSWORTH

122. *"Pure as the snow," we say. Ah! never flake*
Fell through the air
One tenth as fair
As Mary's soul was made for Christ's dear sake.

ELEANOR C. DONNELLY

123. *The life of Mary was such as to be a rule of conduct for all Christians. Her example shows us what we ought to correct, what we ought to avoid, what we ought to do.*

ST. AUGUSTINE

124. *Come ye virgins to a virgin; come, all who conceive, to one who conceived; come, all in labor, to one who was in labor; come, mothers, to a mother.*

ST. FULGENTIUS

125. *When we follow her we do not lose the way; when we pray to her we do not despair; when we think of her we do not go astray. When she holds us we do not fall; when she guides us we do not weary.*

ST. BERNARD

126. *O Mary, your maternal heart embraces sinners despised by the whole world and does not abandon them till they are reconciled to their Judge.*

ST. BONAVENTURE

127. *To all she has opened the breasts of her mercy, that all may be filled out of her abundance; that*

the captive may receive redemption, the sick health, the sad consolation, the sinner pardon, the just grace, the angels joy, the person of her Son, the substance of human flesh, and the whole Trinity, glory.

ST. BERNARD

128. [*She is*]
a safe bridge across the stormy ocean of this life.

ST. PROCULUS

129. *Christ's Mother helps me, else I were too weak.*

Attributed to ST. JOAN OF ARC

130. *The heart of Mary is so kind, so warm, so tender, that those of all mothers united would be but a block of ice compared to hers.*

ST. JOHN BAPTIST VIANNEY
(Curé d'Ars)

131. *What else can I say? She is my Mother.*

ST. STANISLAUS
(upon being asked how much he loved the Blessed Virgin)

132. *Her to aid thee*
When invade thee
Passion's whirlwinds, supplicate.

Medieval MARIALE

133. *Salute Mary, think of Mary, invoke Mary, honor Mary, commend yourselves to Mary, remain with Mary in your house, walk with Mary when you go out. Rejoice with Mary, grieve with Mary, work with Mary, pray with Mary. With Mary carry Jesus in your arms, stand with Mary at the foot of the Cross of Jesus, live and die with Mary and Jesus. Do this and you will live.*

THOMAS A KEMPIS

134. *Arise, Mother of God, and with thy thrilling voice, speak to those who labor with child, and are in pain, till the babe of grace leaps within them.*

JOHN HENRY CARDINAL NEWMAN

135. *The true child of Mary cannot be such unless he attempts in his measure to reproduce in himself her virtues: her devotion to Jesus, her meekness, her simplicity, her modesty, the faith of her who received God's message by the angel without a doubt; her patience, who endured St.*

Joseph's surprise without a word; her obedience, who went up to Bethlehem in the winter, and bore our Lord in the stable; her meditative spirit, who pondered in her heart what she saw and heard about Him; her fortitude, whose heart the sword went through; her self-surrender, who gave Him up during His ministry, and consented to His death; above all . . . her purity, who rather than relinquish her virginity was willing to lose Him as a Son.

JOHN HENRY CARDINAL NEWMAN

136. *O harbinger of day!*
O hope of the pilgrim! lead us still as thou hast led;
in the dark night, across the bleak wilderness,
guide us on to our Lord Jesus, guide us home.

JOHN HENRY CARDINAL NEWMAN

137. *When we don't know where to turn, we turn to her. She can go to the top. Because that spotless girl who knelt in the straw of that stable, looking so pale and so pure in the light of the star, was His Mother, she can go confidently to the throne of God, past the golden halos of the saints, past angels and archangels, past glittering ranks of Cherubim, past Seraphim that veil their faces with their wings. She can*

go right up to the dazzling white throne of God and whisper two words that make all heaven still with breathless awe: "My Son!"

JOSEPH MANTON, C. Ss. R.

138. *Smiling by night upon her sleeping*
children:
O gentle Mary! Our lovely
Mother in heaven!

THOMAS MERTON
(Father M. Louis, O. C. S. O.)

139. *The celestial traitress play,*
And all mankind to bliss betray;
With sacrosanct cajoleries,
And starry treachery of your eyes,
Tempt us back to Paradise.

FRANCIS THOMPSON

140. *Queen of the Angels, Mary, thou whose smile*
Adorns the heavens with their brightest ray;
Calm star that o'er the sea directs the way
Of wandering barks unto their homing isle;
By all thy glory, Virgin without guile,
Relieve me of my grievous woes, I pray!

BOCCACCIO

141. *Virgin, if ever yet*
The misery of man and mortal things
To mercy moved thee, to my prayer incline.
Her I invoke who gracious still replies
To all who ask in faith.

PETRARCH

142. *Unto thy Son say thou that I am His,*
And to me, graceless, make Him gracious.

FRANÇOIS VILLON

143. *In joy and woe, in good and ill,*
Mother of God, be with me still! . . .
Now, when the storms of fate o'ercast
Darkly my present and my past,
Let my future radiant shine
With sweet hopes of thee and thine.

EDGAR ALLEN POE

144. *Who Mary love*
The long year through have Christmas nigh them!

AUBREY DE VERE

145. *My knowledge is so weak, O blissful Queen,*
To tell abroad thy mighty worthiness,

That I the weight of it may not sustain;
But as a child of twelve months old, or less,
That laboreth his language to express;
Even so fare I; and, therefore, I thee pray,
Guide thou my song, which I of thee shall say.

CHAUCER

146. *A servant of Mary will never be lost.*

Attributed to ST. ANSELM

147. *O Mary, console us always, but especially at the hour of our death: come at that last hour and receive our souls, and present them thyself to thy Son, who will judge us.*

ST. BONAVENTURE

148. *Think of me, my dearest Mother, and abandon me not at the hour of my death!*

ST. FRANCIS DE SALES

149. *My children, if you wish for the grace of final perseverance, cultivate great devotion to Mary.*

ST. PHILIP NERI

150. *If all the devils should be arraigned against me before the judgment seat of God; if the whole of hell should rise up against me and open its jaws to devour me; if all the saints should desert me; if thou, O Mary, wouldst only speak one word of intercession I should be saved.*

FRANCISCO SUÁREZ

151. *O, Mary, meet me at the port.*

AN OLD IRISH EJACULATION

152. *Every Hail Mary is a prayer for a happy death. There can be no ending but a happy death for a lifetime of Hail Marys.*

MATTHEW RUSSELL, S. J.

153. *What saidst thou, astronomer,*
When thou didst discover her?
When thy hand its tube let fall,
Thou found'st the fairest Star of all!

FRANCIS THOMPSON

154. *In the garden of God, in the daylight divine,*
Find me a place by thee, Mother of mine.

GERARD MANLEY HOPKINS

155. *Ah, Mary, pierced with sorrow,*
Remember, reach and save,
The soul that stands tomorrow
Before the God that gave.

RUDYARD KIPLING

156. *Every trifling thing is told to her and every great sorrow; she is the sharer of all earth's joys and griefs.*

CARYLL HOUSELANDER

157. [*Mary is*]
the Medicine of Sinners.

ST. EPHREM

158. *If the Son is a King, the Mother who begot Him is rightly and truly considered a Queen and Sovereign.*

ST. ATHANASIUS

159. [*She is a*]
captivator of hearts.

ST. BERNARD

160. *The name of Mary is a key of Heaven. It is uttered, and the portals of Paradise open at the sound.*

ST. BERNARD

161. *O Mary, what must you yourself be, since your name alone is so sweet.*

BLESSED HENRY SUSO

162. *The expansive waters of the ocean are called* Maria (*seas*), *the ocean of graces* Maria.

ST. AUGUSTINE

163. [*Mary is*]
the Star preceding the Sun.

ST. BRIDGET OF SWEDEN

164. *O Mother of the heavenly and earthly Church.*
O Sign of Tranquillity.
O Mother of Orphans.
O Solace of the Wretched.
O Beauty of the World.
O Ladder of Heaven.

FROM THE GAELIC LITANY TO OUR LADY (8th century)

165. *She is called the Star of the Sea because as sailors are guided to their port by the polar star, which is the star of the sea, so also are Christians guided by Mary in the voyage to eternal glory.*

ST. THOMAS AQUINAS

166. *Men sometimes wonder that we call her Mother of life, of mercy, of salvation; what are all these titles compared to that one name, Mother of God?*

JOHN HENRY CARDINAL NEWMAN

167. *As Christ represents humanity in the Redemptive Act, she represents humanity in the co-redemptive act. His suffering was the essential thing, and hers valuable only by derivation. His was the Passion, hers the Com-Passion. He was the Redeemer, but the Church loves to call her Co-Redemptrix.*

FRANK J. SHEED

168. *I think that the whole character of Mary could be summed up by calling her the Loyal Woman.*

MONSIGNOR HUGH F. BLUNT

169. *Speech of an angel shines in the*
waters of her thought like diamonds,
Rides like a sunburst on the
hillsides of her heart.

THOMAS MERTON
(Father Louis, O. C. S. O.)

170. *Gifts and graces flowed upon thee*
In a sweet celestial strife,
And the growing of the Burden
Was the lightening of thy life....
It was Heaven, it was Heaven,
Come before its time to thee.

FATHER FABER
(Frederick William Faber)

171. *He willed the chains of flesh to wear:*
Yet from her arms the worlds He ruled.

AUBREY DE VERE

172. *By the crib of Jesus sleeping,*
Rapt with bliss her quiet watch keeping,
Stood the Mother undefiled.
In her heart what thanks outpouring:
In her heart what love adoring!
As she gazed upon her Child.

STABAT MATER OF THE CRADLE
(Medieval hymn)

173. [*The Virgin's Cradle Hymn:*]
Sleep, sweet Babe! my cares beguiling;
Mother sits beside Thee smiling;
Sleep, my darling, tenderly!
If Thou sleep not, Mother mourneth,

Singing as her wheel she turneth;
Come, soft slumbers, balmily.

SAMUEL TAYLOR COLERIDGE

174. *My God the Baby is*
Who rests upon my knee.
Into those eyes of His
I gaze, mine own to see.

FATHER TABB
(John Bannister Tabb)

175. *And now with wondering eyes and heart I stand*
Before this supreme mystery of Love:
Some kneeling girl with passionless pale face,
An angel with a lily in his hand,
And over both the white wings of a Dove.

OSCAR WILDE

176. [*Mary*]
Who nightly to His cradle crept,
And lying like the moonbeam prone,
Worshiped her Maker as He slept.

AUBREY DE VERE

177. *Joseph did whistle and Mary did sing,*
Mary did sing, Mary did sing,

And all the bells on earth did ring
For joy our Lord was born.

I Saw Three Ships
(Medieval lyric)

178. *Heaven was a-thrill at the thought of it —*
The Hope of the Worlds hidden under her heart!

KATHERINE CONWAY

179. [*The Great Pyramid speaking:*]

A halo mild
Shone from the liquid moon. Beneath her beam
Traveled a tired young Mother and the Child.
Within mine arms she slumbered, and alone
I watched the Infant.

AGNES REPPLIER

180. *Her maternal attentions to the needs of her Child were her worship. She never for an instant lost sight of the Babe in her adoration of her God, nor did her deep realization of the Godhead cause her to forget for a moment the necessities of the Child.*

EDWARD LEEN, C. S. Sp.

181. *I know that at Nazareth, Virgin full of graces,*
You lived in great poverty, not wishing anything more;
No raptures, no miracles, no ecstasies
Embellished your life, O Queen of the elect.

ST. THÉRÈSE OF LISIEUX

182. *Our Lady was a Milkmaid,*
A peasant girl, and poor,
She whom Almighty God obeyed
Would scrub the dairy floor.

HILARY PEPLER

183. *In exaltation and humiliation, in glory and in shame, in joy and in sorrow, she knew but one prayer — that the will of God be done.*

PATRICK AUGUSTINE, CANON SHEEHAN

184. *Every day at Nazareth*
St. Joseph sawed and chipped.
Our Lady bound his finger up
When the chisel slipped.

MARIGOLD HUNT

185. *When Our Lady's little Boy tumbled and grazed*
His knees, what acts of faith she must have made

as she bathed them — faith like that which enabled her to believe, when she saw the Godhead fall beneath the Cross and could not pick Him up.

CARYLL HOUSELANDER

186. *She was the witness of His growth, of His joys, of His sorrows, of His prayers; she was blest with His smile, with the touch of His hand, with the whisper of His affection, with the expression of His thoughts and feelings (for thirty years).*

JOHN HENRY CARDINAL NEWMAN

187. *Because Mary loved more than all,*
She also suffered more than all.

ST. JEROME

188. *She stood gazing with maternal love on the wounds of her Son; she stood, not waiting for Jesus to die, but for the world to be saved.*

ST. AMBROSE

189. *While Jesus was crucified in body,*
Mary was crucified in mind.

ST. LAWRENCE JUSTINIANI

190. *Mary knew martyrdom in her heart.*

ST. BERNARD

191. *Whatever cruelty was inflicted on the martyrs was light, or rather it was nothing compared to the cruelty of Mary's passion.*

ST. ANSELM

192. *Mary's thoughts were not completely absorbed by the sight of the terrible tragedy; at the same time she rejoiced because her only Son was offered in sacrifice for the salvation of mankind.*

ST. PIUS X

193. *Mother of God, He broke thy heart,*
That it might wider be,
That in the vastness of its love
There might be room for me.

FATHER FABER
(Frederick William Faber)

194. *Calvary depicted in its minutest detail was forever before her eyes. The presence of her Divine Son kept it there. Every look at Him was a reminder of it. Every look at His mild, majestic face summoned the ever-present vision of*

that same face, haggard, bloodstained, pale, as it was destined to be on Calvary. Every sound of His voice, speaking from the depths of His great loving Heart, was to the Mother's ears a reminder of the terrible cry of anguish which Jesus would utter when utterly crushed beneath the weight of His Father's vengeance. In very truth it may be said that Mary walked all her life in the shadow of Calvary.

PATRICK AUGUSTINE, CANON SHEEHAN

195. [*It is a Catholic attitude*]
to consider that there is the same virginal spirit of tenderest affection in the Pietà *which we naturally attribute to the Madonna.*

ABBOT VONIER
(Right Reverend Anscar Vonier, O. S. B.)

196. *The star that in His splendor hid her own,*
At Christ's Nativity
Abides — a widowed satellite — alone,
On tearful Calvary.

FATHER TABB
(John Bannister Tabb)

197. *She knew, better than anyone else will ever know it, that the greatest of all griefs is to be unable*

to mitigate the suffering of one whom we love. But she was willing to suffer that, because that was what He asked of her.

CARYLL HOUSELANDER

198. *The first great finding was in the Temple. The second great finding was on Calvary.*

CARYLL HOUSELANDER

199. *If eye hath not seen nor ear heard nor the heart of man understood the reward which God hath prepared for those who love Him, who can tell what He prepared for His Mother, for her who doubtless loved Him more than all others?*

ST. BERNARD

200. [*Mary*]
could not be held down by the shackles of death.

GREGORIAN SACRAMENTARY
(6th century)

201. *Who could believe that the ark of holiness, the dwelling of God, the temple of the Holy Spirit, crumbled into dust. I shudder at the very thought that the virginal flesh of which God was conceived and born, which nourished Him and*

carried Him should have turned to ashes or been given as food to worms.

ST. ROBERT BELLARMINE

202. *It is impossible to imagine of her that she died any other sort of death than one of love — the noblest of deaths for the noblest life that ever was among creatures — a death of which the angels themselves would wish to die, if die they could.*

ST. FRANCIS DE SALES

203. *She died, but her death was a mere fact, not an effect; and when it was over, it ceased to be.*

JOHN HENRY CARDINAL NEWMAN

204. *With no tie upon earth, with her only hope in Heaven; with no remorse for time, with no fear for eternity, dying out of pure love for God, assuredly the death of Mary is a happy one. Here upon earth are tears of sorrow, the only really eloquent testimony of worth appreciated; and Heaven is wild with joy at the prospect of her coming.*

PATRICK AUGUSTINE, CANON SHEEHAN

205. *The Assumption is the Feast of Our Lady's stainless flesh. It proves that flesh is not bad in itself.*

VINCENT McNABB, O.P.

206. *Her appearance was so beautiful and glorious that scarcely anyone could look into her face.*

APOCRYPHAL GOSPEL OF ST. MATTHEW

207. *As our Lord was the most beautiful among the sons of men, Mary was beautiful and fair above all the daughters of Adam.*

ST. ALBERT THE GREAT

208. [*Quoting tradition, our ancestors have said that Our Lady is*]

by nature fairer, more beautiful, and more holy than the Cherubim and Seraphim; she whom all the tongues of Heaven and earth do not suffice to extol.

PIUS IX

209. *Mary's face was most beautiful, but we should not be able to recollect whether it was beautiful or not; we should not recollect any of her features, because it was her beautiful sinless soul which looked through her eyes, and spoke through her mouth and was heard in her voice,*

and compassed her all about; when she was still, or when she walked, whether she smiled, or was sad, her sinless soul — this it was which would draw all those to her who had any grace in them, any remains of grace, any love of holy things. There was a divine music in all she said and did — in her mien, her air, her deportment, that charmed every true heart that came near her.

JOHN HENRY CARDINAL NEWMAN

210. [*Our Lady was*]
young and beautiful, exceedingly beautiful, the like of whom I had never seen.

ST. BERNADETTE
(of Our Lady of Lourdes)

211. *The expression of Our Lady's face was ineffably sweet, tender and compassionate, but what touched me to the very depths of my soul was her glorious smile.*

ST. THÉRÈSE OF LISIEUX
(in describing a vision in her childhood)

212. *So many times we read, in the account of the apparitions of Our Lady, as to St. Bernadette, to the Little Flower, that she* smiled.

MONSIGNOR HUGH F. BLUNT

213. *Now raise thy view*
Unto the visage most resembling Christ.

DANTE ALIGHIERI

214. *Thou, scarcely to be looked upon*
By saints whose footsteps tread the sun.

DANTE ROSSETTI

215. *They served a Maid more beautiful than tongue*
Could tell or heart conceive.

ROBERT SOUTHEY

216. *No one ever knew Christ so profoundly as she did, and no one can ever be a more competent guide and teacher of the knowledge of Christ.*

ST. PIUS X

217. *She was not ignorant of the mystery that she had given birth to a Child who was to rise from the dead.*

ST. AMBROSE

218. [*Our Lady's knowledge was*]
so large, so profound, so diversified, and so thorough that, though she was a poor woman with-

out human advantages, she must, in her knowledge of creation, of the universe, and of history, have excelled the greatest of philosophers, and in her theological knowledge the greatest of theologians, and in her prophetic discernment the most favored of prophets.

JOHN HENRY CARDINAL NEWMAN

219. *Her wisdom is not her own, but His to whom we beg her to lead us.*

BEDE JARRETT, O. P.

220. *Herself a thinker, the Virgin exacts long thought from those who would know her.*

JEAN GUITTON

221. *My children, help me to combat the evils of the Church and of society, not with the sword but with the Rosary.*

PIUS IX

222. *We most earnestly exhort all the faithful to persevere devoutly in the daily recitation of the Rosary.*

LEO XIII

223. *If you wish to convert anyone to the fullness of the knowledge of our Lord and of His Mystical Body, then teach him the Rosary. One of two things will happen. Either he will stop saying the Rosary — or he will get the gift of faith.*

MOST REVEREND FULTON J. SHEEN

224. *I'll give my jewels for a set of beads.*

SHAKESPEARE

225. *There is one harp that any hand can play*
And from its strings what harmonies arise! . . . .
When on their beads our Mother's children pray,
Immortal music charms the grateful skies.

JOYCE KILMER

226. *That as Christ first came to us through Mary, so too His second coming will be preceded by an age of Mary.*

Prediction of ST. LOUIS MARIE GRIGNON DE MONTFORT

INDEX OF AUTHORS QUOTED

(Arabic numerals below refer to numbered sections, not pages, of the book.)

SUBJECT-MATTER INDEX